RUTH

Rescued by the Redeemer

6 STUDIES FOR INDIVIDUALS OR GROUPS

LifeGuide®
BIBLE STUDIES

DALE LARSEN AND SANDY LARSEN

IVP Connect

An imprint of InterVarsity Press
Downers Grove, Illinois

InterVarsity Press
P.O. Box 1400, Downers Grove, IL 60515-1426
ivpress.com
email@ivpress.com

InterVarsity Press® is the book-publishing division of InterVarsity Christian Fellowship/USA®, a movement of students and faculty active on campus at hundreds of universities, colleges and schools of nursing in the United States of America, and a member movement of the International Fellowship of Evangelical Students. For information about local and regional activities, visit intervarsity.org.

All Scripture quotations, unless otherwise indicated, are taken from THE HOLY BIBLE, NEW INTERNATIONAL VERSION®, NIV® Copyright © 1973, 1978, 1984, 2011 by Biblica, Inc.™ Used by permission. All rights reserved worldwide.

Cover image: © Cath Waters / Trevillion Images

ISBN 978-0-8308-3109-8 (print)
ISBN 978-0-8308-6427-0 (digital)

Printed in the United States of America ∞

 As a member of the Green Press Initiative, InterVarsity Press is committed to protecting the environment and to the responsible use of natural resources. To learn more, visit greenpressinitiative.org.

P	20	19	18	17	16	15	14	13	12	11	10	9	8	7	6	5
Y	33	32	31	30	29	28	27	26	25	24	23	22	21	20		

Contents

Contents

Getting the Most
Out of *Ruth*

Who can read only *part* of the book of Ruth? The narrative holds us in suspense as it propels us through a series of crises where the future of the central characters hangs in the balance. Every section of the book ends in a cliffhanger. We *have* to keep reading to find out what happens next.

Many Bible studies of the book of Ruth focus on the life and character of Ruth herself. *Ruth* takes a more comprehensive view of the book as a whole. While the book is named for Ruth, and she is prominent in the action, other significant players populate the drama: Naomi, Elimelek, Mahlon, Kilion, Orpah, Boaz, an unnamed guardian-redeemer, reapers, elders, neighbors. All have their share of importance in the historical narrative.

The unknown author of Ruth was a master storyteller. The book is carefully and deftly constructed. Like any well-told story, it contains conflict, but not the classic clash of good versus evil. One commentator notes how the lack of stereotypical conflict in the book plays up the personal qualities of the characters:

> There is no villain in the story. No reprehensible act is done by any character. But the author has used detail and

contrast to such good effect that the difference between
ordinary and exceptional goodness stands out clearly
against the background of details of common life. Orpah
is in no way lacking in dutiful devotion. She is ready to accompany her mother-in-law to a new country, and yields
only to a second urging of Naomi to go back to her own
people (1:8-14). The nearer kinsman is prepared to accept
his responsibility and redeem the property, and yields
only when he finds that a marriage is involved which may
conflict with his duty to his own inheritance (4:4-6). It is
against this background that the unusual magnanimity of
Ruth and Boaz is seen in its true perspective.*

In the midst of the various players in the story and above
them all is the chief character, the sovereign God "under whose
wings" Ruth comes to take refuge (Ruth 2:12). The Lord is the
one making things happen in the human and natural world. Yet
his intervention is subtle, never blatantly obvious. Key events
in the book appear to be flukes of coincidence. Why is there
a truce between Moab and Israel at this time? Why do both
Mahlon and Kilion die in Moab? Why do both die childless?
Why do Ruth and Naomi arrive in Bethlehem precisely when
they do? Why does Ruth just happen to glean in a field belonging to Boaz? Only by a thorough reading of the book do we
see how surely God has superintended the events that lead to
Ruth's eventual place in the lineage of Christ.

What does the book of Ruth have to do with us today? Although Ruth and Boaz are mentioned in the New Testament
only in Matthew's genealogy of Jesus (Matthew 1:5), Christians
have long seen in the book of Ruth a foreshadowing of our redemption through Christ. As Ruth and Naomi were destitute,
with no status and no hope, we were in spiritual poverty and
could not rescue ourselves. Like them, we were in need of a

guardian-redeemer who would come to our aid. As Boaz in love intervened and took responsibility to save Ruth and Naomi, Christ in love has become our ultimate Redeemer who assumes the burden of our need and gives us a place in his kingdom.

To set up the historical context of Ruth, our study begins with the book of Judges. It is an understatement to say that during this time Israel was spiritually and politically unstable. The Israelites were absorbed in doing whatever each person thought best, with little regard for what the Lord thought best. For several hundred years the nation spiraled through idolatry, judgment, crying out for help, deliverance and another fall into idolatry. The only constant was the Lord's merciful concern for his people and his determination to preserve the line of his eventual Guardian-Redeemer, Jesus the Messiah.

In the midst of the chaos of the book of Judges, the book of Ruth emerges as a bright island of faithfulness and hope. All those cliffhangers are resolved in joyful redemption and a future that reaches into the New Testament and beyond.

Suggestions for Individual Study

1. As you begin each study, pray that God will speak to you through his Word.

2. Read the introduction to the study and respond to the personal reflection question or exercise. This is designed to help you focus on God and on the theme of the study.

3. Each study deals with a particular passage so that you can delve into the author's meaning in that context. Read and reread the passage to be studied. The questions are written using the language of the New International Version, so you may wish to use that version of the Bible. The New Revised Standard Version is also recommended.

4. This is an inductive Bible study, designed to help you dis-

cover for yourself what Scripture is saying. The study includes
three types of questions. Observation questions ask about the
basic facts: who, what, when, where and how. Interpretation
questions delve into the meaning of the passage. Application
questions help you discover the implications of the text for growing in Christ. These three keys unlock the treasures of Scripture.

Write your answers to the questions in the spaces provided
or in a personal journal. Writing can bring clarity and deeper
understanding of yourself and of God's Word.

5. It might be good to have a Bible dictionary handy. Use it to
look up any unfamiliar words, names or places.

6. Use the prayer suggestion to guide you in thanking God
for what you have learned and to pray about the applications
that have come to mind.

7. You may want to go on to the suggestion under "Now or
Later," or you may want to use that idea for your next study.

Suggestions for Members of a Group Study

1. Come to the study prepared. Follow the suggestions for
individual study mentioned above. You will find that careful
preparation will greatly enrich your time spent in group discussion.

2. Be willing to participate in the discussion. The leader of
your group will not be lecturing. Instead, he or she will be encouraging the members of the group to discuss what they have
learned. The leader will be asking the questions that are found
in this guide.

3. Stick to the topic being discussed. Your answers should be
based on the verses that are the focus of the discussion and not
on outside authorities such as commentaries or speakers. These
studies focus on a particular passage of Scripture. Only rarely
should you refer to other portions of the Bible. This allows for

everyone to participate in in-depth study on equal ground.
4. Be sensitive to the other members of the group. Listen attentively when they describe what they have learned. You may be surprised by their insights! Each question assumes a variety of answers. Many questions do not have "right" answers, particularly questions that aim at meaning or application. Instead the questions push us to explore the passage more thoroughly. When possible, link what you say to the comments of others. Also, be affirming whenever you can. This will encourage some of the more hesitant members of the group to participate.

5. Be careful not to dominate the discussion. We are sometimes so eager to express our thoughts that we leave too little opportunity for others to respond. By all means participate! But allow others to also.

6. Expect God to teach you through the passage being discussed and through the other members of the group. Pray that you will have an enjoyable and profitable time together, but also that as a result of the study you will find ways that you can take action individually and/or as a group.

7. Remember that anything said in the group is considered confidential and should not be discussed outside the group unless specific permission is given to do so.

8. If you are the group leader, you will find additional suggestions at the back of the guide.

---

*Dorothea Ward Harvey, "Ruth, Book of," *Interpreter's Dictionary of the Bible*, ed. George A. Buttrick et al. (Nashville: Abingdon, 1962), 4:133.

1

Redeemer Rejected

Judges 2:6—3:6

A friend who is of Sandy's generation recalls the transformation when his family's rural home was finally electrified. In the entire house there were exactly four bare light bulbs, all dangling from cords with pull chains and no shades. The change felt miraculous. Our friend's family thought they had arrived. No more kerosene lamps for them!

How can people who have grown up in a brilliantly illuminated world comprehend the darkness of rural homes before electric wires reached them? For younger people, such persistent darkness has never existed. Surely the older generation are the ones who most appreciate having electricity in their homes, for they remember life without it.

GROUP DISCUSSION. How much do you know about life as your grandparents lived it? How well can you describe their daily life?

PERSONAL REFLECTION. What are some perils of a lack of knowledge of the past?

The opening words of the book of Ruth are "In the days when the judges ruled." To understand the context of Ruth, it makes sense to explore what things were like in Israel at that time. After the death of Moses, Joshua assumed the leadership of Israel. The people entered Canaan and began the conquest of the land God had promised them; however, they did not drive out all the pagan inhabitants of the land. *Read Judges 2:6-15.*

---

1. This Scripture passage describes a period of transition in the history of Israel. What changes occurred during this time (vv. 6-10)?

---

2. In only a couple of generations, the Israelites basically forgot the Lord and all he had done for Israel (v. 10). Why do you think such a radical change took place?

---

3. What evidence do you see of similar change happening in our society today?

4. What were the consequences of Israel's forsaking the Lord (vv. 11-15)?

Read Judges 2:16-19.

5. Identify all the expressions of God's mercy that you find in this passage.

6. Trace the destructive cycle Israel fell into during this time.

7. Verse 17 contains strong language: the people "prostituted themselves to other gods." Such imagery of idol worship as prostitution is repeated throughout the Old Testament. Why is prostitution an apt image for idolatry?

8. In what ways are we tempted to sell ourselves into forms of idolatry, that is, to worship false gods in order to gain personal benefit?

9. How can Christians today avoid Israel's destructive cycle of calling out to God for rescue and then falling back into idolatry?

Read Judges 2:20–3:6.

10. How would the Lord use the other nations in the life of Israel (2:21-22; 3:1-4)?

11. What were the eventual results of Israel's continued disobedience (3:5-6)?

12. Look back at your response to question 8. Now make it more personal by identifying an area where you are tempted or have even "sold yourself" to an idol in order to gain something.

13. Consider the cost of recommitting yourself to the Lord in the area you identified in question 12. What step(s) will you take to let go of that idol?

Pray that you will surrender idols and that you will stay alert to any further encroachment of idols into your life.

Now or Later

- Has your life ever resembled, or does it now resemble, Israel's pattern of idolatry, judgment, pleading for help, deliverance and another fall into idolatry? Draw a representation of that pattern. Place words or symbols along the way to show what was happening in your life at each point. If the pattern has been broken, write a prayer of thanks to the Lord. If the pattern is persisting, write a prayer asking the Lord to break this pattern and put you on a new path of obedience and commitment to him.

- Scan the book of Judges, taking note of each deliverer and how he or she delivered Israel. Which deliverers strike you as especially interesting? Unlikely? Admirable? And why?

2

A Radical Decision

Neither of us can forget the moment we decided to go into writing full-time. We had gone through several years of frustrating job searches, trying to land "ideal" situations. Nothing had worked out. Meanwhile we were both getting more and more freelance writing assignments for several Christian publishers. One day after a particularly disheartening job turndown, Dale said, "Why don't we forget it all and just go write?" Sandy thought it was the greatest idea she'd ever heard. While the decision meant stepping out into unknown territory with no material security, it also meant relief, excitement, expectancy and hope.

GROUP DISCUSSION. People make radical life changes for various reasons. What are some of those reasons? Delve into your own experience and that of people you know.

PERSONAL REFLECTION. Recall a time when you were in a period of transition, one that you did not initiate. Did you welcome it as a challenge? Become overwhelmed with anxiety? Hold your breath (figuratively speaking) until it was over? Respond in some other way?

"The days when the judges ruled" (Ruth 1:1) were the approximately three centuries between Israel's entrance into Canaan and the anointing of their first king. Judges 17:6 (see also Judges 21:25) sums up the period: "In those days Israel had no king; everyone did as they saw fit" or "every man did that which was right in his own eyes" (KJV). The recurring pattern we saw in session 1 was idolatry, divine judgment, crying out to the Lord, divine deliverance and a prompt return to idolatry. The book of Ruth shows that even in such a spiritually unstable society, some people saw fit to practice faithfulness and compassion. *Read Ruth 1.*

1. Six people are identified by name in chapter 1. What series of events concentrates the narrative to only two (Naomi and Ruth) by the end of the chapter?

2. Imagine that you are standing by the side of the road and overhear the conversation in verses 8-18. What emotions do you hear expressed, and in what tones of voice?

3. Why does Naomi keep urging her daughters-in-law to stay in Moab (vv. 8-13)?

4. Both Orpah and Ruth take decisive actions. Why do you think each decides as she does?

5. What personal qualities does Ruth display here? Consider especially verses 14-18.

6. From a worldly perspective, how is Orpah's decision a sensible one (vv. 14-15)?

7. If Ruth goes with Naomi, what life changes will she need to accept (vv. 16-17)?

8. Throughout the chapter, how is the Lord acknowledged as involved in these events? Note especially verses 6, 8-9, 13, 16-17, 20-21.

9. How have you seen the same pattern of the Lord's involvement in your own life?

10. When Naomi and Ruth enter Bethlehem—Ruth as a new resident, Naomi as a returnee—what are their greatest needs?

11. What reasons do they have to be hopeful?

12. Consider ways the Lord might be calling you to exercise faith and make a change in your life. What are your fears about making a change?

13. What reasons do you have to be hopeful in the face of change?

Pray for courage to face the risks of following the Lord.

Now or Later

- Do you know someone who has made a radical life change to follow Christ? If possible, ask that person what went into the decision, what the costs have been, and what has made the decision worth the costs.
- Read a biography of someone who gave up financial success, status, worldly power or perhaps even physical life to follow Christ. Pay particular attention to the person's reasons and what made the sacrifices worth it.

3

Newfound Hope

Ruth 2

Tara's grief was almost unendurable. Within ten days both her husband and her baby daughter died. Trying to make sense of it all, she began to be drawn to a life of faith, although she did not know what kind of faith it would be. A friend mentioned Tara's situation to another friend, who then asked the people of her church to pray. Tara's explorations into faith led to reading the Bible, and eventually she became a Christian believer.

Years later, knowing nothing of the connection, Tara met and married one of the men from the church that had prayed for her. She also discovered that three of the women in her prayer group had been in that church and had prayed for her.

Tara writes, "In 1997, when I was an agnostic widow living in New Jersey, a group of Christians in Massachusetts had been praying for me. And while my own attempts to find a faith never adequately explained my conversion, this did. I had been prayed into the kingdom."*

GROUP DISCUSSION. When has the Lord brought just the right person or circumstances into your life when you least expected it?

PERSONAL REFLECTION. Faced with a difficult situation, how do you judge whether the Lord wants you to wait and see what he brings into your life, or whether to go ahead and take action?

The law of Moses decreed that when grain and vineyards were harvested, part of the produce should be left for the poor and foreigners to gather for themselves (Leviticus 19:9-10; 23:22; Deuteronomy 24:19-22). Ruth knows of this law, and now she proposes to take advantage of the opportunity to glean in the fields. *Read Ruth 2.*

1. Trace the steps of how the lives of Ruth and Boaz become intertwined in this chapter.

2. When Ruth takes the initiative to go out and glean, her action leads her to Boaz's field. In your own life, when has a step forward in faith brought even better results than you anticipated?

3. In verses 4-16, what qualities do you see in the character of Boaz?

4. How has Ruth's reputation paved the way for Boaz's positive impression of her (vv. 6-7, 11-12)?

5. Consider your own reputation. What expectations do you think a stranger would have of you, based on what others have said about you?

6. How does Boaz show increasing kindnesses to Ruth (vv. 8-9, 14-16)?

7. Why is Ruth surprised at Boaz's kindnesses (vv. 10, 13)?

8. In many senses Ruth could be considered a nobody. In what way(s) have you felt like you were a nobody?

---

9. We have no precise metric equivalent of an *ephah* (v. 17), but the best information is that it was three-eighths to two-thirds of a bushel. An ephah of threshed barley would weigh about thirty-five pounds. Imagine yourself as Ruth carrying home a sack of that much barley. What are you feeling physically and emotionally?

---

10. Verse 20 is a turning point in the story, when new possibilities open up. How does the revelation of Boaz's identity magnify the significance of what Ruth has been doing?

---

11. What new possibilities have you seen the Lord opening up in your own life lately?

12. Ruth accepts Boaz's offer (v. 21) and continues to glean throughout the barley and wheat harvests for a period of two or three months. How will you pursue the new possibilities the Lord is opening up for you?

Pray that your eyes will be open to godly possibilities as the Lord brings new people and new circumstances into your life.

Now or Later

• Naomi identifies Boaz as a guardian-redeemer (Ruth 2:20). Study the roles of the guardian-redeemer in the law of Moses in these passages:

   Deuteronomy 25:5-10

   Leviticus 25:25-28, 47-49

• Journal about times when you realized that a seeming coincidence was actually the Lord at work.

---

*Tara Edelschick, "A Grief Transformed," *Christianity Today*, July/August 2014, pp. 95-96.

4

A Bold Appeal Rewarded

Some years after we taught English in Ukraine, a former student contacted us with exciting news—and an outlandish request. For the coming year he would be a Fulbright Visiting Scholar at the University of California at Berkeley. He had learned that rents in that area were sky-high. Could we find him a low-cost place to live in Berkeley? Preferably with a Christian roommate?

We had always said we would do anything for our Ukrainian students, but this was impossible. We lived in Illinois and knew no one in Berkeley, California. One conceivable contact occurred to us. The ministry International Students, Inc., must have a chapter at UC Berkeley. Through the ISI website we contacted the local staff member and almost apologetically relayed our friend's request. The ISI staffer sent out an appeal to his local supporters, and within hours a Christian family responded. They would be happy to host our friend rent free for the year he was teaching there. They even lived right on a bus line to campus.

A bold, even presumptuous, request fulfilled in one day! The

Lord not only provided for our student; he gave us robust evidence that he could meet any need.

GROUP DISCUSSION. What is the most bold and even brazen request anyone has ever made of you? How did you react?

PERSONAL REFLECTION. When have you deliberately done something that observers could take the wrong way? Why did you proceed in spite of the possible negative interpretations?

Since the return from Moab, Naomi has appeared to be a passive participant in events. Now she shows that she can formulate a shrewd plan to insure Ruth's future. *Read Ruth 3.*

1. The events of this chapter take place over only a few hours, from one day until early the next morning. What elements give this part of the story such intensity?

2. How do you weigh the dangers versus benefits of a risky action?

3. As Boaz had warned (Ruth 2:8-9), women were vulnerable working in the fields, even in daytime with other people around. Yet Naomi sends Ruth alone at night to the threshing floor where the men are celebrating the harvest, and Ruth agrees to go. What do you think gives both women the confidence that this is a wise and ultimately safe action to take?

4. What is at stake here for Naomi? That is, what could she lose?

5. What is at stake here for Ruth? That is, what could she lose?

6. Compare Naomi's instructions (vv. 3-4) with Ruth's actions at the threshing floor (vv. 7-9). How does Ruth go beyond what Naomi has instructed her to do?

7. When Boaz realizes Ruth is there, he can react in various ways. What does his response to her presence reveal about his character (vv. 10-11)?

8. Boaz was a person of standing in the Bethlehem community (Ruth 2:1). How might he jeopardize his social status by marrying a Moabite woman?

9. What potential snag arises in the plan (vv. 12-13)?

10. Even while their relationship is still unsettled, how does Boaz protect and provide for Ruth (vv. 14-15)?

11. Verses 4, 13 and 18 portray Boaz as a decisive person. What would happen if the guardian-redeemer were indecisive?

12. How do all three participants in these matters—Naomi, Ruth and Boaz—show that they trust each other?

13. What decision(s) are you facing now that would call for decisive and even daring action?

14. What are you willing to risk in order that the Lord's will should be accomplished in your life?

Pray that what you request, whether from the Lord or from other people, will be in alignment with what the Lord wants.

• Divide a piece of paper into three columns headed "Boaz," "Ruth" and "Naomi." Under each name, list the values that were important to each of these three people based on what we have read so far in Ruth. Circle the values that seem most prominent. Draw a square around the values that you also hold important.

• Study the following incidents in which women boldly approached Jesus:

Mark 5:24-34: woman with the flow of blood

Mark 7:24-30: Gentile woman whose daughter was demon-possessed

Luke 7:36-50: woman of bad reputation at Pharisee's home

Mark 14:3-9: woman who anointed Jesus at Bethany (revealed to be Mary in John 11:1-2)

○ For each case, respond to these questions:

1. Why and how did the woman approach Jesus?

2. What obstacles did she overcome in order to approach him?

3. What was the outcome?

5

The Redeemer Acts

Ruth 4:1-12

The long-expected letter or email has finally arrived. You know the message holds news about your future. It will tell you if the job is yours, or if you got the loan, or if you won the scholarship, or if your audition was successful, or if you were admitted to the program of your dreams. But you can't bring yourself to open the message. You delay and delay. While the suspense is killing you, the prospect of disappointment is worse. What a helpless feeling to know that your future lies in someone else's hands! Or does it? Such nail-biting, breath-holding times test a believer's trust that the future is in the hands of our sovereign God.

GROUP DISCUSSION. How would you advise someone who is facing the anxiety of a particularly uncertain future?

PERSONAL REFLECTION. How well do you handle uncertainty?

At this point Ruth and Naomi temporarily disappear from the book of Ruth. No doubt they are somewhere on the sidelines and keenly aware of what is going on. *Read Ruth 4:1-12.*

1. Describe the setting of this passage: Where does it happen and who is involved in the action?

2. Recall a time when an important matter in your life depended on someone else's decision. If you prayed during that time, what did you pray for? If you did not pray but had hopes, what did you hope for?

3. The passage begins with "Meanwhile," referring to Ruth and Naomi's early morning discussion in Ruth 3:16-18. What does the fact that Boaz has already started to take action reveal about his character?

4. How does Boaz carefully set the scene for his encounter with the rival guardian-redeemer (vv. 1-2)?

5. If you were Boaz, how do you think you would be praying at this point?

6. Boaz has every reason to regard the nearer guardian-redeemer as his personal rival and an obstacle to his aims. How does Boaz still show respect and tact in approaching the other man (vv. 1-4)?

7. Boaz does not immediately reveal the details of the proposed transaction, but does so gradually (vv. 4-5). Why is this a wise approach?

8. Neither Ruth nor Naomi appears in this exchange. Apparently they are not present or at least are not close enough to be conspicuous. Wherever they are while Boaz meets with the other guardian-redeemer, what do you think each woman is thinking and praying?

9. At first the next-in-line guardian-redeemer is willing to fulfill his responsibilities and redeem the land. Why does he change his mind (vv. 5-6)?

---

10. Boaz acknowledges, even announces, that any child he has with Ruth will carry on Mahlon's name rather than his own (v. 10). This is in accordance with the law of levirate marriage (Deuteronomy 25:5-6). The prospect of jeopardizing his inheritance is precisely what made the other guardian-redeemer *refuse* to marry Ruth (v. 6). Why do you think Boaz is willing to jeopardize his own inheritance in this way?

---

11. Boaz accepted the role of guardian-redeemer. How has Christ acted as Guardian-Redeemer for you?

---

12. In verses 7-12 the transaction is publicly confirmed by witnesses. Why would their validation be important?

13. Throughout this transaction, how do Boaz's words and actions affirm Ruth's value as a person and a member of Bethlehem society?

14. Naomi and Ruth must have breathed sighs of relief when they heard the guardian-redeemer's decision and Boaz's declaration (vv. 8-10). Consider uncertainties you are facing right now. What encouragement can you draw from how events worked out for Ruth and Naomi?

Pray about uncertainties you are now experiencing. Commit them to the Lord and ask for his help to trust him and to be free from worry.

Now or Later

• Study any of these New Testament references of Jesus Christ as Redeemer or Ransomer (the list is not exhaustive):

 Matthew 20:26-28; Mark 10:43-45

 Romans 3:22-24; 8:22-23

 1 Corinthians 1:30

 Ephesians 1:7-8; 4:30

 1 Timothy 2:5-6

 Titus 2:11-14

Hebrews 9:11-12, 15

1 Peter 1:18-19

- Journal about how Jesus has acted as Guardian-Redeemer for you. Write a prayer, song or poem of thanks to him.
- Choose some object as a symbol of a particular difficulty that you have consciously committed to God. Place the object where you will see it often, as a reminder that you have entrusted this problem to the Lord.

6

An Improbable Ancestor

**Ruth 4:13-22;
Matthew 1:1-6**

Family trees can be hard to verify. A particularly vexing complication in the United States is that immigrants' names have often been changed. Sometimes the original names were too hard for Americans to pronounce, sometimes immigrants wanted to establish a new identity in a new world, and sadly sometimes new names and identities were forced on them.

When Dale's great-grandfather arrived from Copenhagen, Denmark, his last name was Andersen. Supposedly he changed his name to Larsen because there were too many Andersens. The explanation doesn't make a lot of sense because there must have been just as many Larsens as Andersens on the boat, but that is the family story. It would be futile to try to trace Dale's Danish ancestors by searching for Larsens in Copenhagen.

The family tree of the Messiah, the Son of David, was never subject to whimsical name changes or a desire to escape prior associations. The Holy Spirit directed Jesus' family line before and after King David. With Jesus there can be no question of mistaken identity.

GROUP DISCUSSION. We have seen God working in Ruth's time to put events in place which would eventually result in the incarnation of the Son of God. Throughout human history, God has been working to fulfill his purposes in the world, although his working was not (and is not now) always obvious or easy to discern. Do you see God working today to fulfill his purposes for the future, and if so, how?

PERSONAL REFLECTION. What are some ways the Lord has intervened to change your life for the better? Think of internal as well as external changes.

After all the cliffhangers and the crises where events could have taken an unhappy turn, life at last is good for Naomi, Ruth and Boaz. Yet the story is far from finished. *Read Ruth 4:13-22.*

1. Identify the ways in which Ruth's life has changed since the beginning of the book.

2. At the time of Naomi's return to Bethlehem, she described her life as *bitter* and herself as *empty* (Ruth 1:20-21). What is different about Naomi and her situation now?

3. Instead of *bitter* and *empty*, what words do you think Naomi might now use to describe herself (vv. 14-16)?

4. Throughout the book of Ruth, the Lord has been working behind the scenes; his interventions have been implied but seldom overtly acknowledged. Now we are told of Ruth that "the LORD enabled her to conceive, and she gave birth to a son" (v. 13). The Hebrews knew that God is the ultimate cause of any child being conceived, so why might the writer single out God's involvement in the conception of this particular child?

5. As a result of Boaz's willingness to act as guardian-redeemer, what current and future blessings does he receive?

6. In verses 11-12, the witnesses express hopes, which are fulfilled in verses 18-22. When and how has the Lord, your Redeemer, unexpectedly fulfilled your hopes?

The next Scripture skips ahead about a thousand years. The line of Ruth and Boaz has continued through King David all the way to Jesus Christ, who is born in Bethlehem, the hometown of Naomi and Boaz. *Read Matthew 1:1-6.*

---

7. Compare the genealogy in Matthew 1:2-6 with the genealogy in Ruth 4:18-22. How do they match up?

---

8. In Matthew's genealogy of Jesus, only four women other than Mary are mentioned (vv. 3-6). All four seem unlikely candidates to enter the family line of the Messiah.

Why do you think these women are specifically identified in Jesus' ancestry?

- *Tamar.* Judah's first two sons married Tamar, and both died. Judah's third son should have married his brothers' widow, but Judah feared for his son's life and connived to keep the marriage from happening. Tamar disguised herself as a prostitute and seduced Judah, as a result conceiving Perez (Genesis 38:1-30).

- *Rahab.* Rahab was a Gentile prostitute (or possibly the proprietor of a house of prostitution) in Jericho. She concealed the Israelite spies because she knew that the Lord had given Canaan to Israel. As the spies promised her, she and her

family were spared when the Israelites conquered Jericho
(Joshua 2:1-24; 6:22-25).

- *Ruth.* As we have seen, she was a foreigner from a pagan land
  traditionally at odds with Israel.

- *Bathsheba, Uriah's wife.* David overstepped his authority as
  king and committed adultery with the wife of Uriah, one of
  his best fighting men. To account for Bathsheba's pregnancy,
  David ordered Uriah killed in battle and quickly married
  Bathsheba. That child died; their next child was Solomon
  (2 Samuel 11:1–12:25).

---

9. Matthew 1:5 reveals that Boaz was a son of Rahab—yes, *that*
Rahab, the Canaanite prostitute who hid the Israelite spies in
Jericho. How might this fact have affected the attitude of Boaz,
and the attitudes of people in his hometown of Bethlehem,
toward Gentile foreigners and their fitness to be joined with
God's people, the Jews?

10. How do you see yourself as an unlikely candidate to be part of God's kingdom?

---

11. Ruth was a nobody who came to a strange country with nothing; yet she played a significant role in God's redemption of the world. Where do you see your place in God's plan of redemption?

---

12. What is the next step you need to take in fulfilling your place in God's redemptive plan for the world?

Thank God for how he has worked out his purposes and continues to work out his purposes in the world and specifically in your own life. Pray for trust and confidence that he is still working. Pray that you will always be a willing part of his plans.

Now or Later

Journal, and then discuss with one or more other believers, how you can reflect the redemptive life of Christ in whatever areas of life you find yourselves: business, education, home, family, community, volunteer work, missions close to home, missions in distant areas.

Leader's Notes

MY GRACE IS SUFFICIENT FOR YOU. (2 COR 12:9)

Leading a Bible discussion can be an enjoyable and rewarding experience. But it can also be *scary*—especially if you've never done it before. If this is your feeling, you're in good company. When God asked Moses to lead the Israelites out of Egypt, he replied, "O Lord, please send someone else to do it!" (Ex 4:13). It was the same with Solomon, Jeremiah and Timothy, but God helped these people in spite of their weaknesses, and he will help you as well.

You don't need to be an expert on the Bible or a trained teacher to lead a Bible discussion. The idea behind these inductive studies is that the leader guides group members to discover for themselves what the Bible has to say. This method of learning will allow group members to remember much more of what is said than a lecture would.

These studies are designed to be led easily. As a matter of fact, the flow of questions through the passage from observation to interpretation to application is so natural that you may feel that the studies lead themselves. This study guide is also flexible. You can use it with a variety of groups—student, professional, neighborhood or church groups. Each study takes forty-five to sixty minutes in a group setting.

There are some important facts to know about group dynamics and encouraging discussion. The suggestions listed below should enable you to effectively and enjoyably fulfill your role as leader.

Preparing for the Study

1. Ask God to help you understand and apply the passage in your own life. Unless this happens, you will not be prepared to lead others. Pray too for the various members of the group. Ask God to open your hearts to the message of his Word and motivate you to action.

2. Read the introduction to the entire guide to get an overview of the entire book and the issues that will be explored.

3. As you begin each study, read and reread the assigned Bible passage to familiarize yourself with it.

4. This study guide is based on the New International Version of the Bible. It will help you and the group if you use this translation as the basis for your study and discussion.

5. Carefully work through each question in the study. Spend time in meditation and reflection as you consider how to respond.

6. Write your thoughts and responses in the space provided in the study guide. This will help you to express your understanding of the passage clearly.

7. It might help to have a Bible dictionary handy. Use it to look up any unfamiliar words, names or places. (For additional help on how to study a passage, see chapter five of *How to Lead a LifeGuide Bible Study,* InterVarsity Press.)

8. Consider how you can apply the Scripture to your life. Remember that the group will follow your lead in responding to the studies. They will not go any deeper than you do.

9. Once you have finished your own study of the passage, familiarize yourself with the leader's notes for the study you are leading. These are designed to help you in several ways. First, they tell you the purpose the study guide author had in mind when writing the study. Take time to think through how the study questions work together to accomplish that purpose. Second, the notes provide you with additional background information or suggestions on group dynamics for various questions. This information can be useful when people have difficulty understanding or answering a question. Third, the leader's notes can alert you to potential problems you may encounter during the study.

10. If you wish to remind yourself of anything mentioned in the leader's notes, make a note to yourself below that question in the study.

Leading the Study

1. Begin the study on time. Open with prayer, asking God to help the group to understand and apply the passage.

2. Be sure that everyone in your group has a study guide. Encourage the group to prepare beforehand for each discussion by reading the introduction to the guide and by working through the questions in the study.

3. At the beginning of your first time together, explain that these studies are meant to be discussions, not lectures. Encourage the members of the group to participate. However, do not put pressure on those who may be hesitant to speak during the first few sessions. You may want to suggest the following guidelines to your group.

☐ Stick to the topic being discussed.

☐ Your responses should be based on the verses that are the focus of the discussion and not on outside authorities such as commentaries or speakers.

☐ These studies focus on a particular passage of Scripture. Only rarely should you refer to other portions of the Bible. This allows for everyone to participate in in-depth study on equal ground.

☐ Anything said in the group is considered confidential and will not be discussed outside the group unless specific permission is given to do so.

☐ We will listen attentively to each other and provide time for each person present to talk.

☐ We will pray for each other.

4. Have a group member read the introduction at the beginning of the discussion.

5. Every session begins with a group discussion question. The question or activity is meant to be used before the passage is read. The question introduces the theme of the study and encourages group members to begin to open up. Encourage as many members as possible to participate, and be ready to get the discussion going with your own response.

This section is designed to reveal where our thoughts or feelings need to be transformed by Scripture. That is why it is especially important not to read the passage before the discussion question is asked. The passage will tend to color the honest reactions people would otherwise give because they are, of course, supposed to think the way the Bible does.

You may want to supplement the group discussion question with an icebreaker to help people to get comfortable. See the community section of *Small Group Idea Book* for more ideas.

You also might want to use the personal reflection question with your group. Either allow a time of silence for people to respond individually or discuss it together.

6. Have a group member (or members if the passage is long) read aloud the passage to be studied. Then give people several minutes to read the passage again silently so that they can take it all in.

7. Question 1 will generally be an overview question designed to briefly survey the passage. Encourage the group to look at the whole passage, but try to avoid getting sidetracked by questions or issues that will be addressed later in the study.

8. As you ask the questions, keep in mind that they are designed to be used just as they are written. You may simply read them aloud. Or you may prefer to express them in your own words. There may be times when it is appropriate to deviate from the study guide. For example, a question may have already been answered. If so, move on to the next question. Or someone may raise an important question not covered in the guide. Take time to discuss it, but try to keep the group from going off on tangents.

9. Avoid answering your own questions. If necessary, repeat or rephrase them until they are clearly understood. Or point out something you read in the leader's notes to clarify the context or meaning. An eager group quickly becomes passive and silent if they think the leader will do most of the talking.

10. Don't be afraid of silence. People may need time to think about the question before formulating their answers.

11. Don't be content with just one answer. Ask, "What do the rest of you think?" or "Anything else?" until several people have given answers to the question.

12. Acknowledge all contributions. Try to be affirming whenever possible. Never reject an answer. If it is clearly off-base, ask, "Which verse led you to that conclusion?" or again, "What do the rest of you think?"

13. Don't expect every answer to be addressed to you, even though this will probably happen at first. As group members become more at ease, they will begin to truly interact with each other. This is one sign of healthy discussion.

14. Don't be afraid of controversy. It can be very stimulating. If you don't resolve an issue completely, don't be frustrated. Move on and keep it in mind for later. A subsequent study may solve the problem.

15. Periodically summarize what the group has said about the passage. This helps to draw together the various ideas mentioned and gives continuity to the study. But don't preach.

16. At the end of the Bible discussion you may want to allow group members a time of quiet to work on an idea under "Now or Later." Then discuss what you experienced. Or you may want to encourage group members to work on these ideas between meetings. Give an opportunity during the session for people to talk about what they are learning.

17. Conclude your time together with conversational prayer, adapting the prayer suggestion at the end of the study to your group. Ask for God's help in following through on the commitments you've made.

18. End on time.

Many more suggestions and helps are found in *How to Lead a LifeGuide Bible Study.*

Components of Small Groups

A healthy small group should do more than study the Bible. There are four components to consider as you structure your time together.

Nurture. Small groups help us to grow in our knowledge and love of God. Bible study is the key to making this happen and is the foundation of your small group.

Community. Small groups are a great place to develop deep friendships with other Christians. Allow time for informal interaction before and after each study. Plan activities and games that will help you get to know each other. Spend time having fun together going on a picnic or cooking dinner together.

Worship and prayer. Your study will be enhanced by spending time praising God together in prayer or song. Pray for each other's needs and keep track of how God is answering prayer in your group. Ask God to help you to apply what you are learning in your study.

Outreach. Reaching out to others can be a practical way of applying what you are learning, and it will keep your group from becoming self-focused. Host a series of evangelistic discussions for your friends or neighbors. Clean up the yard of an elderly friend. Serve at a soup kitchen together, or spend a day working on a Habitat house.

Many more suggestions and helps in each of these areas are found in *Small Group Idea Book*. Information on building a small group can be found in *Small Group Leaders' Handbook* and *The Big Book on Small Groups* (both from InterVarsity Press). Reading through one of these books would be worth your time.

Study 1. Redeemer Rejected. Judges 2:6–3:6.

Purpose: To take steps to avoid the destructive cycle of idolatry into which Israel fell during the period of the judges.

Question 1. Joshua and his generation died, and a new generation grew up who did not know the Lord or the history of what he had done for Israel. The people began to worship the gods of Canaan. "Baal and the Ashtoreths" (v. 13) refers to male and female deities of fertility. Israel's history was slave labor in Egypt and nomadic life in the desert. As they began to settle in the land and practice agriculture, they must have craved the supposed advantages of cultivating the favor of gods who could guarantee good harvests and productive flocks and herds.

Question 5. The Hebrew term *judge*

describes an individual who maintains justice for the tribes of Israel. The justice comes in bringing protection from foreign oppressors. Maintaining international justice was often the role of the king. What made these judges unlike kings was that there was no formal process for assuming the office, nor could it be passed on to one's heirs. There was no supporting administration, no standing army and no taxation to underwrite expenses. So while the actual function of the judge may have had much in common with the king, the judge did not enjoy most of the royal prerogatives. . . . The judges did not serve as heads of government in general but did have the authority to call out the armies of the tribes. Prior to the monarchy, no one from any one tribe would have been able to exercise such authority over another tribe. God was the only central authority. Therefore, when a judge successfully rallied the armies of several tribes, it was seen as the work of the Lord through that judge (see 6:34-35). (John H. Walton, Victor H. Matthews and Mark W. Chavalas, *IVP Bible Background Commentary: Old Testament* [Downers Grove, IL: InterVarsity Press, 2000], p. 246)

Question 6. Israel's destructive cycle was oppression by enemies, crying out to the Lord for rescue, deliverance by the Lord through a judge, a temporary return to the Lord, death of the judge and falling back into idolatry. Note that the record shows no repentance for idolatry, only relief at deliverance. The lack of genuine repentance explains why the people reverted so quickly to worshiping false gods. In Judges 10:6-16 we see what appears to be genuine repentance and turning away from idols, but such repentance is rare in Judges.

Question 7. Prostitutes sell their bodies for money, food or some other benefit. The Israelites sold themselves to idols; they offered worship and sacrifices in order to get something in return. For example, they worshiped fertility gods in order to get bountiful harvests.

Question 9. Israel cried to the Lord for help but failed to repent of their idolatry and abandon false gods once and for all. If we pray to the Lord for help in times of distress but don't genuinely turn to him in our hearts and forsake false gods, we are sure to revert to our idols, whatever they are.

Question 11. Mingling and intermarrying with the pagan inhabitants of Canaan, with the resultant lapse into idolatry, continued to be a persistent problem in Israel. Even kings fell prey to the temptation, most notably Solomon (1 Kings 11:1-13).

The eventual result of chronic idolatry was foreign exile: Israel to Assyria, and later Judah to Babylon. Even after the Jews returned to their land, intermarriage with pagans caused serious problems (Ezra 9–10).

Study 2. A Radical Decision. Ruth 1.
Purpose: To examine and appreciate the daring nature of Ruth's decision to go to Israel with Naomi.
Question 1. The famine of Ruth 1:1 is not recorded in the book of Judges, but it could have been a result of God's judgment. Apparently this was a time of peace between Israel and Moab, although the two nations had never lived comfortably together.

When Elimelek took his family and left Israel for Moab, it was not the ideal action of a faithful Jew.

For Israel, Moab was known for several things, none of them good. The Moabites had originated out of an incestuous relationship between Lot and his older daughter (Gen. 19:30-38); their king Balak had hired Balaam to curse Israel when they came out of Egypt (Num. 22–24); their women had been a stumbling block to Israel in the wilderness, seducing them to the worship of false gods (Num. 25); and they had recently oppressed the Israelites in the days of Eglon (Judg. 3). Does this sound like the place to go in order to raise a godly family? (Iain M. Duguid, *Esther & Ruth* [Philipsburg, NJ: P&R, 2005], p. 132)

From the order of names in verses 2-4, it would seem that Ruth's husband was Kilion; however, Ruth 4:10 reveals that Ruth's husband was Mahlon.
Question 3. Naomi's hypothetical marriage and sons (v. 11) reflect the law of levirate marriage (Deut 25:5-6). If a man died without a son, his brother was to marry the dead man's widow. If they then had a son, that son was considered the offspring and heir of the deceased brother. Genesis 38:6-11 shows that

the practice predated the Mosaic law. But because Naomi has no more sons, she believes that Orpah and Ruth will remain childless if they accompany her to Israel.

Question 7. In verse 16, Ruth acknowledges and embraces three major life changes: place, society and religion. She can physically leave her former place and her former society, but to leave her religion will require an internal change; she could still carry on her native religion in her heart. The Moabite national god was Chemosh; the Moabites are identified as the "people of Chemosh" in Numbers 21:29. Chemosh is called "the detestable god of Moab" (1 Kings 11:7) and "the vile god of Moab" (2 Kings 23:13)—although he was not vile or detestable enough to keep Solomon from erecting a shrine to Chemosh for Solomon's pagan wives (1 Kings 11:7). Chemosh made severe demands of his worshipers. Mesha, king of Moab, sacrificed his own son on the city wall as an appeal to the god to gain victory over Israel (2 Kings 3:26-27).

Question 11. Naomi had heard that the famine was over (v. 6). The sight of the barley harvest in progress (v. 22) confirmed the report.

Study 3. Newfound Hope. Ruth 2.
Purpose: To discern the hand of the Lord in Ruth and Naomi's transformation from despondency to hope.

Question 2. The agricultural year in Israel offered extended opportunities for gleaning.

> Olives were harvested at the beginning of the year—i.e., the middle of September to the middle of November, by beating the trees with long sticks (Deut 24:20; Isa 17:6). In March-April flax was harvested by cutting it off near the ground, then laying the stalks out to dry (Josh 2:6). The harvesting of barley took place in April or early May, while the wheat harvest occurred in May-June. During August-

September the summer fruits—figs, grapes, and pomegran-
ates—were harvested. (H. Neil Richardson, "Harvest," *Interpreter's Dictionary of the Bible*, ed. George A. Buttrick et
al. [Nashville: Abingdon, 1969], 2:527)

Question 8. Ruth was a Gentile foreigner, an outsider to the
covenant people of God. Specifically she was a native of Moab,
a longstanding enemy of Israel. She was a woman in a male-
dominated society. She had no parents (at least not in Israel),
no husband and no children to provide for her. She lived with
another widow, her older mother-in-law, and no male family
member was providing for them. Ruth was a person without
standing in Israelite society.

Question 10. For the first time in the book of Ruth, verse 20
introduces the idea of a guardian-redeemer. In Scripture "redemption means deliverance from some evil by payment of a
price. It is more than simple deliverance." Common to all uses
of the word *redemption* is "the idea of freedom secured by payment of a price." (L. L. Morris, "Redeemer, Redemption," *New
Bible Dictionary*, ed. D. R. W. Wood, 3rd ed. [Downers Grove,
IL: InterVarsity Press, 1996], p. 1003)

The guardian-redeemer was specifically responsible for
protecting the interests of needy members of the extended
family—e.g., to provide an heir for a brother who had
died (Dt 25:5-10), to redeem land that a poor relative had
sold outside the family (Lev 25:25-28), to redeem a relative who had been sold into slavery (Lev 25:47-49) and
to avenge the killing of a relative (Nu 35:19-21; "avenger"
and "kinsman-redeemer" are translations of the same Hebrew word). (Marvin R. Wilson and John H. Stek, note to
Ruth 2:20 in *NIV Study Bible*, 10th Anniversary Edition
[Grand Rapids: Zondervan, 1995], p. 364)

The kinsman-redeemer was a near blood-relative and
always male. This near-kinsman (or one of them, if many)

had a duty to protect his weaker relatives. He had to redeem property belonging to relatives when they had to sell
land or goods (Lev 25:23-25) and even their persons when
they had sold themselves into slavery (Lev 25:47-55). For
example, Jeremiah bought land belonging to his cousin at
Anathoth because he was the kinsman-redeemer (Jer 32).
In the case of Ruth, it was important that the nearer relative give up his right/duty in favor of Boaz (Ruth 4:6). The
kinsman-redeemer was also duty bound to come to the de-
fense or aid of a relative in either a legal or an actual strug-
gle. . . . The duty of the kinsman also extended to the levirate, the begetting and raising of children with the wife of
a deceased brother so as to carry on his name (cf. the case
of Tamar, Gen 38; see also Deut 25:6; Ruth 2:20; 4:1-6). . . .
The near-relative might also act as an avenger, the avenger
of blood being guiltless when executing the killer of a relative, provided the killer had not lawfully sought refuge in
one of the six designated cities (Num 35:9-34; Deut 19:1-
13). Finally, it was the duty of the kinsman to take the side
of his relative in a court action. . . . All these concepts of
a duty to aid and rescue reflect, through their metaphoric
application, the relationship of God and Christ with a believer. However, the notion is not clearly presented in the
NT, save in the function of Redeemer. ("Legal Images,"
Dictionary of Biblical Imagery, ed. Leland Ryken, James C.
Wilhoit and Tremper Longman III [Downers Grove, IL:
InterVarsity Press, 1998], p. 501)

Study 4. A Bold Appeal Rewarded. Ruth 3.
Purpose: To take courage and act decisively when God asks us
to go out on a limb for his purposes.
Question 3. Threshing is the separation of heads of grain from
the rest of the plant. Harvested stalks of grain were laid out on

a threshing floor and beaten with flails or trod on by animals. Once separated, the loose grains still had to be winnowed from the chaff. Winnowing was often done in the late afternoon, when the breeze had picked up after the day's heat. The process used a pronged fork on a long handle by which the threshed grain was tossed into the air. The breeze blew the lighter chaff a short distance away (it was later retrieved to be used as fodder), while the grain fell back to the threshing floor. The threshing floor was usually out in an open area to make maximum use of the breeze. (John H. Walton, Victor H. Matthews and Mark W. Chavalas, *IVP Bible Background Commentary: Old Testament* [Downers Grove, IL: InterVarsity Press, 2000], p. 279)

Question 6. "Ruth uses a phrase that elsewhere is used to refer to betrothal and marriage. It is also clear from Boaz's response in the next verse that she has requested marriage. Naomi had not advised her to be this bold, but the outcome of marriage was certainly what Naomi had in mind" (ibid., pp. 279-80).

Ruth immediately made her objective clear when she requested, "Spread the corner of your garment over me." She was using the accepted idiom meaning "Marry me." . . . The gesture is a symbol of protection as well as a declaration that the man is willing to enter into sexual consummation with his chosen partner.

Boaz had prayed in Ruth 2:12 that Ruth might be rewarded by the Lord under whose wings she had taken refuge. Ruth now essentially asked Boaz to answer his own prayer, for "garment-cover" and "wing" are from a similar root in Hebrew.

Ruth's reason for this action is expressed in her appeal to Boaz as a "kinsman-redeemer." That is a legal status. Under Jewish law, then, her request was not particularly unusual. (Walter C. Kaiser et al., *Hard Sayings of the Bible* [Downers Grove, IL: InterVarsity Press, 1996], pp. 197-98)

Question 8. We saw in session 1 that intermarriage with foreigners had been disastrous for Israel (Judg 3:5-6). The residents of Bethlehem certainly knew the stigma associated with marriage outside the covenant people of Israel. However, they also knew of Ruth's admirable character and that she had clearly and publicly renounced her pagan roots and put her faith in the Lord (Ruth 2:11-12).

Study 5. The Redeemer Acts. Ruth 4:1-12.
Purpose: To face uncertainty with the confidence that the Lord is working out his will for our good and his honor.
Question 4. The *IVP Bible Background Commentary: Old Testament* informs us that

> The gate area in Israelite cities was an open space that was the hub of activity. Merchants, visitors, messengers and judges all frequented that area and conducted their business there. . . . Numerous excavations have produced gate plans showing that often there were benches lining the whole area where people could meet for various purposes. . . . The elders, usually clan leaders or heads of household, served as the governing body of the city. Judicial and legal matters were in their hands. Here there is no legal judgment to pass, but they would oversee the legal transaction to assure that all was done according to law and custom, as well as serve as witnesses to the transaction. (John H. Walton, Victor H. Matthews and Mark W. Chavalas, *IVP Bible Background Commentary: Old Testament* [Downers Grove, IL: InterVarsity Press, 2000], p. 280)

Question 6. Sandy once participated in a study of the book of Ruth with a number of farmers' wives. The writer of the study guide contended that the book of Ruth was a cobbled-together collection of several fictional stories. As evidence, the writer pointed out that Naomi was supposedly destitute, yet she was a property owner. When the farm women heard that idea, they laughed. Didn't the study writer know that farmers are routinely land rich and cash poor? Even in poverty, Naomi would hesitate to sell a piece of land that was her inheritance. While Naomi and Ruth had returned to Bethlehem at the wrong season to plant a crop, the land would be a productive resource in the future.

Question 9. Ruth's deceased husband, Mahlon, had been the rightful heir to the land, which is why the guardian-redeemer would acquire Mahlon's widow. If Ruth then had a son, he would be considered Mahlon's heir.

Question 11. The New Testament never cites the book of Ruth or draws a parallel between Boaz and Christ. Yet it seems perfectly appropriate to see Christ as the ultimate Guardian-Redeemer who loves us, intervenes to rescue us, assumes the burden of our need and gives us a place in his kingdom.

Question 12. The witnesses mention Rachel, Leah, Perez and Tamar (vv. 11-12). Rachel and Leah were the two wives of Jacob (Israel). Along with their servants Bilhah and Zilpah, they were the mothers of the twelve sons of Jacob whose descendants became the twelve tribes of Israel (Genesis 29:1–30:24; 35:16-26). Perez was the son of Judah by his daughter-in-law Tamar, the result of a double deception that will be explored in more detail in session 6. Despite the unhappy circumstances of Perez's conception (Genesis 38:1-30), he is honored here as the ancestor of Boaz.

Study 6. An Improbable Ancestor.
Ruth 4:13-22; Matthew 1:1-6.
Purpose: To be willing to be used of God for his purposes, as he has used many unlikely people throughout human history.
Question 4. Ruth had no children with her first husband,

Mahlon, in perhaps ten years of marriage (Ruth 1:4-5). Possibly her ability to conceive now is viewed as miraculous. In any case, God had a special purpose for this child as the eventual grandfather of King David.
Question 5. In the short term, Boaz is joined in marriage with the woman he loves, and they soon have a son. They enjoy abundant support and approval from the Bethlehem community. Long-term, Boaz becomes an ancestor of the Messiah, Jesus Christ. Along with Ruth and Naomi, Boaz's name has a permanent place in Jewish history and ultimately in the history of God's redemptive work in the world.

Dale and Sandy Larsen are writers living in Rochester, Minnesota. They have authored over thirty Bible studies, including more than ten LifeGuide® Bible Studies.

Other LifeGuides®
from Dale and Sandy Larsen

Couples of the Old Testament
978-0-8308-3048-0

Faith
978-0-8308-3081-7

Growing Older & Wiser
978-0-8308-3044-2

Hosea
978-0-8308-3041-1

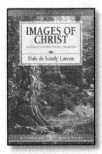

Images of Christ
978-0-8308-3002-2

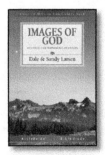

Images of God
978-0-8308-3001-5

Images of the Spirit
978-0-8308-3035-0

What should we study next?

We have LifeGuides for . . .

Knowing Jesus
Advent of the Savior
Following Jesus
I Am
Abiding in Christ
Jesus' Final Week

Knowing God
Meeting God
God's Comfort
God's Love
The 23rd Psalm
Miracles

Growing in the Spirit
Meeting the Spirit
Fruit of the Spirit
Spiritual Gifts
Spiritual Warfare

Looking at the Trinity
Images of Christ
Images of God
Images of the Spirit

Developing Disciplines
Christian Disciplines
God's Word
Hospitality
The Lord's Prayer
Prayer
Praying the Psalms
Sabbath
Worship

**Deepening
Your Doctrine**
Angels
Christian Beliefs
The Cross
End Times
Good & Evil
Heaven
The Kingdom of God
The Story of Scripture

Seekers
Encountering Jesus
Jesus the Reason
Meeting Jesus

Leaders
Christian Leadership
Integrity
Elijah
Joseph

**Shaping Your
Character**
Christian Character
Decisions
Self-Esteem
Parables
Pleasing God
Woman of God
*Women of the
New Testament*
*Women of the
Old Testament*

**Living Fully
at Every Stage**
Singleness
Marriage
Parenting
*Couples of the
Old Testament*
*Couples of the
New Testament*
*Growing Older
& Wiser*

**Reaching
Our World**
Missions
Evangelism
Four Great Loves
Loving Justice

Living Your Faith
Christian Virtues
Forgiveness

**Growing in
Relationships**
Christian Community
Friendship